ALL ABOUT INSECTS

ALL ABOUT FLIES

by Golriz Golkar

Ideas for Parents and Teachers

Pogo Books let children practice reading informational text while introducing them to nonfiction features such as headings, labels, sidebars, maps, and diagrams, as well as a table of contents, glossary, and index.

Carefully leveled text with a strong photo match offers early fluent readers the support they need to succeed.

Before Reading

- "Walk" through the book and point out the various nonfiction features. Ask the student what purpose each feature serves.
- Look at the glossary together. Read and discuss the words.

Read the Book

- Have the child read the book independently.
- Invite him or her to list questions that arise from reading.

After Reading

- Discuss the child's questions. Talk about how he or she might find answers to those questions.
- Prompt the child to think more. Ask: Have you ever seen a fly? Where was it? What was it doing?

Pogo Books are published by Jump!
5357 Penn Avenue South
Minneapolis, MN 55419
www.jumplibrary.com

Library of Congress Cataloging-in-Publication Data

Names: Golkar, Golriz, author.
Title: All about flies / by Golriz Golkar.
Description: Minneapolis, MN: Jump!, Inc., [2025]
Series: All about insects | Includes index.
Audience: Ages 7-10
Identifiers: LCCN 2023052591 (print)
LCCN 2023052592 (ebook)
ISBN 9798889969877 (hardcover)
ISBN 9798889969884 (paperback)
ISBN 9798889969891 (ebook)
Subjects: LCSH: Flies—Juvenile literature.
Classification: LCC QL533.2 .G65 2025 (print)
LCC QL533.2 (ebook)
DDC 595.77–dc23/eng/20231109
LC record available at https://lccn.loc.gov/2023052591
LC ebook record available at https://lccn.loc.gov/2023052592

Editor: Katie Chanez
Designer: Emma Almgren-Bersie

Photo Credits: Paulrommer SL/Shutterstock, cover; cookelma/iStock, 1; phichak/Shutterstock, 3; Ale-ks/iStock, 4; Ton Bangkeaw/Shutterstock, 5; Peter Vahlersvik/iStock, 6-7; Paul Broadbent/Alamy, 8; Andrea Geiss/Shutterstock, 9; Víctor Suárez/Alamy, 10-11; Ray Wilson/Alamy, 12-13; Shelli Jensen/Shutterstock, 14-15; Cathy Keifer/Shutterstock, 16; rakijung/iStock, 17; peter bocklandt/iStock, 18-19; imageBROKER.com GmbH & Co. KG/Alamy, 20-21; Protasov AN/Shutterstock, 23.

Printed in the United States of America at Corporate Graphics in North Mankato, Minnesota.

TABLE OF CONTENTS

CHAPTER 1

HI, LITTLE FLY!

An **insect** lands. It has six legs. Two **antennas** help it smell. So do hairs on its body. Two large eyes help it spot food. Wings allow it to fly. What is this insect? It is a fly!

Around 125,000 fly **species** live around the world. Houseflies live near humans. Why? They eat waste humans leave behind.

Flies have tiny hairs on their feet. These make a kind of glue. This helps flies stick to surfaces. They climb up, down, sideways, and even upside down!

TAKE A LOOK!

What are the parts of a fly? Take a look!

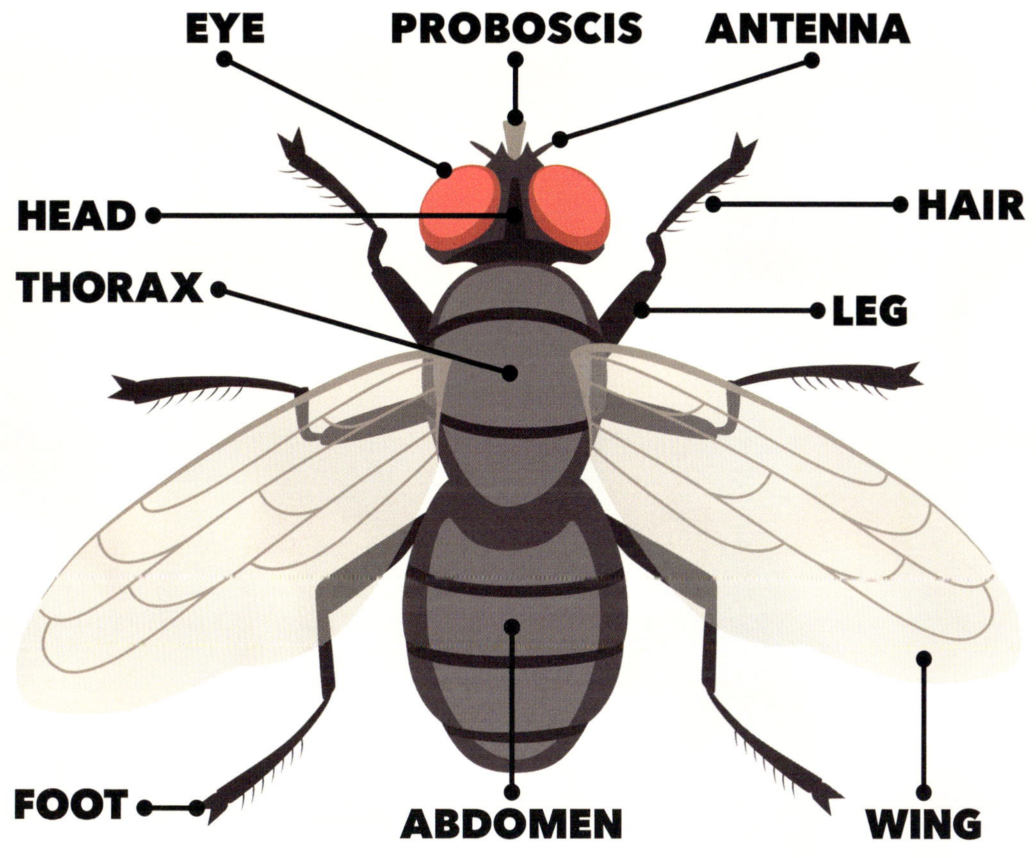

CHAPTER 2

LIFE CYCLE

Flies start their lives as eggs. Females lay more than 100 white eggs at a time. They lay them on rotting food. Why? This will be food for the **larvae** when they hatch.

After less than one day, the eggs hatch. White larvae come out. They are also called maggots. They eat. They **molt** many times.

After less than one month, a larva crawls to a cool place. It grows a case. It turns into a **pupa**. Inside, its body changes.

pupa

In less than one month, the fly pushes out of the case. It is now an adult. It has wings and big eyes. A female's eyes are far apart. A male's eyes almost touch.

TAKE A LOOK!

Flies grow in four stages. Take a look!

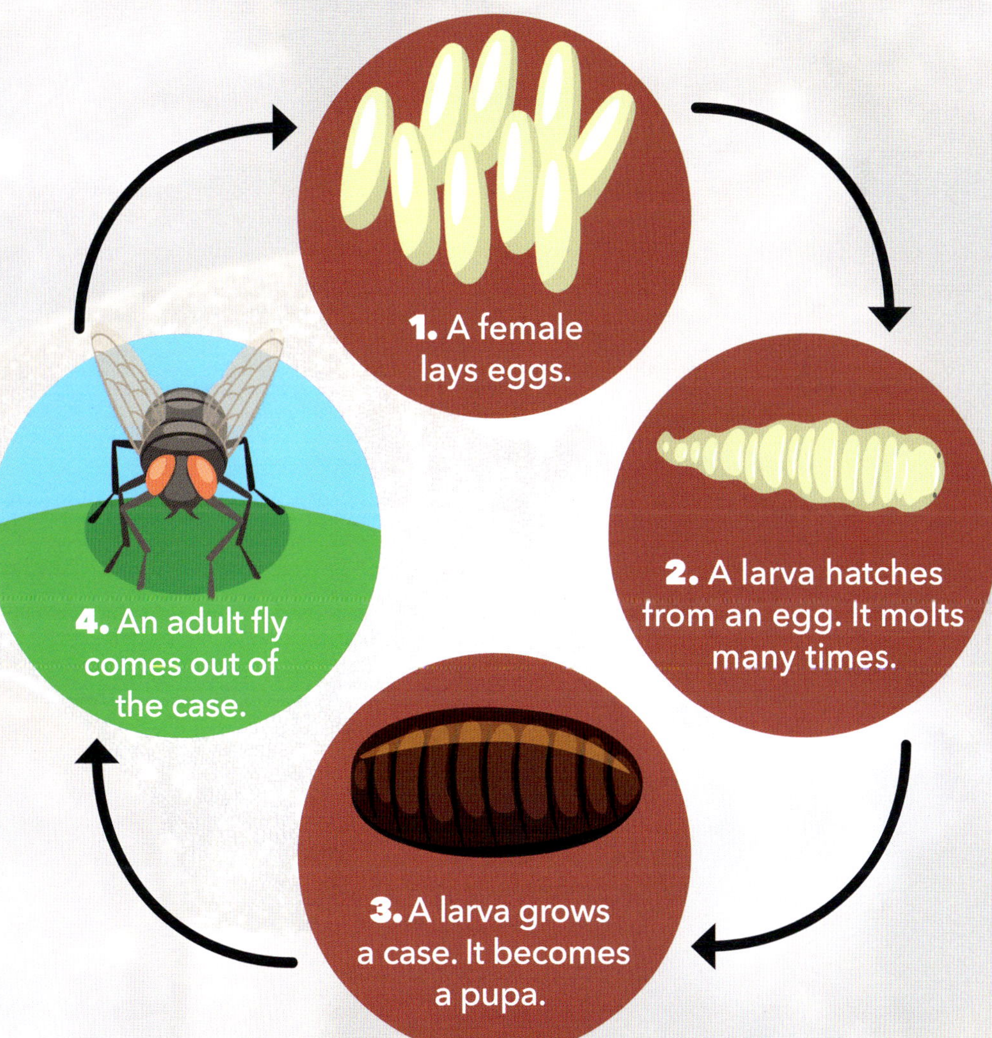

Adult flies live for about 30 days. In that time, they eat and **mate**. Females lay eggs.

DID YOU KNOW?

A female fly can lay up to 1,000 eggs in her lifetime.

CHAPTER 3

FLY FOOD

Flies are an important part of the **food chain**. They are **prey** for **predators** like frogs, spiders, birds, and lizards. Some fish eat flies that buzz above water.

Flies rest at night. During the day, they look for food. They walk on food. Why? They taste with their feet!

Flies eat ripe fruits and vegetables. Some like vinegar and candy. They even eat animal waste.

Most flies do not bite or chew. They throw up **saliva** onto food. This turns the food into liquid. Then they drink it with their **proboscis**!

DID YOU KNOW?

Horseflies live near people. They are big. Female horseflies bite. Ouch!

proboscis

Flies see much better than humans. Big eyes help them see all around. They can even see behind them. They fly fast to avoid danger. Have you ever tried to catch a fly?

DID YOU KNOW?

Flies are **pests**. Why? They carry diseases. Flies should be kept away from food people eat.

ACTIVITIES & TOOLS

TRY THIS!

PAPER FLY

Make a housefly in this fun activity!

What You Need:

- 2 sheets of black construction paper
- scissors
- pencil
- 3 black pipe cleaners
- glue
- 1 sheet of white paper
- tape
- big googly eyes

1. **Cut a large oval lengthwise out of one sheet of black construction paper. This is the body.**
2. **Cut the other sheet of construction paper in half. On one half, draw a circle. Cut it out. This is the head.**
3. **Glue the head to the body.**
4. **Cut each pipe cleaner in half to make six pieces. Tape three pieces to each side of the body. Bend the pieces to look like fly legs.**
5. **Draw two wings on the white paper. Cut them out. Glue the wings to the body.**
6. **Glue the googly eyes to the top of the head. Now you have a fly!**

GLOSSARY

antennas: Feelers on the head of an insect.

food chain: An ordered arrangement of animals and plants in which each feeds on the one below it in the chain.

insect: A small animal with three pairs of legs, one or two pairs of wings, and three main body parts.

larvae: Insects in the stage of growth between eggs and pupae.

mate: To come together to produce babies.

molt: To shed an old, outer skin so that a new one can grow.

pests: Insects or animals that interfere with human activity.

predators: Animals that hunt other animals for food.

prey: Animals that are hunted by other animals for food.

proboscis: A long, tubelike mouthpart that helps flies suck liquids.

pupa: An insect in the stage of growth between larva and adult.

saliva: A substance made by the body that helps break down food.

species: One of the groups into which similar animals and plants are divided.

INDEX

TO LEARN MORE

Finding more information is as easy as 1, 2, 3.

1. Go to www.factsurfer.com
2. Enter "flies" into the search box.
3. Choose your book to see a list of websites.